Religions

in the Republic of China

Religions

in the Republic of China

**Compiled by the Government Information Office
Republic of China**

GIO photo archives

Religions in the Republic of China on Taiwan

Publisher: C. J. (Chien-jen) Chen
Published by the Government Information Office
2 Tientsin Street, Taipei, Taiwan, ROC
http://www.gio.gov.tw

Printed by Yu Hwa Art Printing Co., Inc.
95-8 Pao Chung Road, Hsintien,
Taipei County, Taiwan, ROC

Designer: Amy Chang

1st edition, D5 October 1998
Catalog Card No.: GIO-EN-BL-87-058-I-1
ISBN 957-02-2706-0

Printed in the Republic of China
Price: NT$100, US$3.0

Contents

HUANG Chung-hsin

HUANG Chung-hsin

Preface

As Article 13 of the ROC Constitution guarantees the freedom of religion, it is an organic right possessed by all people on the ROC. Therefore, worshipers of officially recognized religions can freely congregate, hold religious services, and proselytize, as long as they act within the bounds of the law.

Taiwan has created an economic miracle from its limited natural resources, land, and population. It has also implemented the first democratic and free political system in the five-thousand years of Chinese history. After attaining democracy and affluence, the people of Taiwan have turned to raising their level of spiritual consciousness and fulfilling their higher aspirations. This spiritual revitalization has been led by President Lee Teng-hui. As a result, proselytizing and other activities by various religions are common. Here in the Republic of China, different religions have co-existed in harmony, with people showing great tolerance and acceptance for all religions, both local and foreign.

Religious groups have traditionally been the backbone of community service in Taiwan. Aside

from sharing a common concern for the poor and needy, religious organizations have also diversified into medical services, such as free health checkups, health awareness campaigns, and visiting the sick at homes and in hospitals. A 1997 statistics shows that religious groups were operating 52 hospitals, 70 clinics, 25 centers for the retarded, 13 retirement homes, 11 orphanages, 7 welfare institutions for the handicapped, and 4 rehabilitation centers. Besides social services, religious organizations have also played an important role in education as exemplified by the 45 universities and colleges, 40 high schools, 21 elementary schools, and 455 kindergartens that they have established.

More than half (11.8 million) the residents of Taiwan follow one of thirteen registered religions on the island, and their numbers are growing every year. These religions include Buddhism, Taoism, Catholicism, Protestantism, Hsuan-yuan Chiao, Islam, Li-ism, Tenrikyo, Baha'i, T'ienti Teachings, Tien Te Chiao, I-kuan Tao, and Mahikarikyo.

Monks of the Fokuangshan Temple and former KMT secretary-general,
Wu Poh-hsiung, lead Buddhist faithfuls in a welcoming ceremony for one of the few
remaining Buddha's teeth to Taiwan.

Buddhism

Buddhism is a pan-Asian religion which originated in India and spread to China sometime during the first century A.D. Buddha was an Indian prince named Siddhartha Gautama, who renounced his royal heritage and luxurious lifestyle in search of spiritual understanding and release from the suffering of this world. It is said that he achieved enlightenment through self-denial and meditation, and thereafter instructed his followers on the nature of dharma, the true way. Buddha's teachings focus around the "Four Noble Truths." The first two are that life is fundamentally difficult and disappointing and that suffering is the result of desire. To cease these negative feelings, one must therefore learn to control desire; to control one's desire, one should correct the errors in one's ways such as intentions, speech, conduct, lifestyle, thoughts, and concentration.

A lotus blossom or water lily symbolizing the Buddhist paradise, or "pure land."

A Chinese Buddha image.

Site of the "million Buddhas" at Kaohsiung's Fokuangshan Temple.

An elder monk instructs initiates on Buddhist liturgies and discipline.

Buddhism spread south to Ceylon, Cambodia, and Laos to become Theravada or Hinayana (Little Vehicle) and north to China, Korea, and Japan, where it developed into Mahayana (Great Vehicle). Hinayana is concerned more with individual salvation through contemplation and self-purification, while Mahayana puts greater emphasis on compassion and universal salvation.

An example of Chinese temple architecture.

Mahayana presupposes a life of suffering, many powerful godlike figures, and the possibility of transcending to a higher state of being. Several of its tenets are similar to those of Taoism and the folk religion widely accepted in China. As a result, Mahayana Buddhism has become the most popular form of Buddhism in China, and, indeed, in all of Northeast Asia.

Although Buddhism originated in India, since its introduction to China almost two millennia ago during the reign of Emperor Ming Ti (around 65 A.D.), it has been thoroughly Sinified. In terms of thought, canons, and ceremonies, the Buddhism practiced in China today is distinctly Chinese, and few Chinese people consider it a foreign religion.

Buddhist prayer books and rosaries.

Meditation is becoming popular in Taiwan's increasingly hectic society.

Buddhism was introduced to Taiwan in the late 16th century. By the time Ming loyalist Koxinga escaped to Taiwan and drove out the Dutch, Buddhist monks were already coming to Taiwan. Buddhist temples were built with the support of Koxinga and his followers. By the 17th century, Buddhist temples had been erected by officials, the gentry, and local people; however, Buddhist missionary work at the time was limited. Some Buddhist temples were also used for folk religion, and thus received popular support.

The Japanese brought their forms of Buddhism to Taiwan when they gained Taiwan as an indemnity at the turn of the 20th century. Representatives of eight Buddhist sects, namely, the Tendai, the Shingon, the Pure Land, the Soto, the Rinzai, the Shin, the Nichiren, the Hokke, and the Agon, came to Taiwan to proselytize. Already established

Buddhist sects responded to the incursion by accommodating the newcomers. By 1925, a large number of monks from Japan were in leading positions in local Buddhist temples. Buddhism in Taiwan gradually took on a Japanese cast, particularly in the areas of moral and disciplinary codes and education.

During the Japanese occupation, Buddhist groups in Taiwan separated into northern, central, and southern schools. The monk Shan-hui founded the Yueh-mei Mountain school of Keelung (the northern school), as the monk Chueh-li established the Fa-yun Szu school of Miaoli (the central school)

A Buddhist prayer congregation held at Fokuangshan Temple.

Believers on a pilgrimage recite sutras and chant songs.

and the Kai-yuan Szu school of Tainan (the southern school).

Elementary students practice meditation at a Buddhist retreat camp.

In 1947, Master Chang-chia established the Buddhist Association of the ROC in Nanking. As the ROC central government relocated to Taiwan, large numbers of monks followed it, establishing the Taiwan provincial chapter of this organization.

Post-war Buddhism in Taiwan has witnessed the re-establishment of the Chinese Mahayana tradition, the renewed stress on moral and disciplinary codes, and the ceremony of ordination. Furthermore, emphasis has been put on Buddhist educa-

A Buddhist publication.

tion, the establishment of Buddhist institutes, and active proselytization.

Since 1980, Tantric Buddhism, an esoteric sect which developed between the second and fourth century A.D. in India, has become increasingly popular in Taiwan. In recent years, exiled Tibetan monks of this sect have come to Taiwan, rapidly attracting a large following and commanding a significant influence on the religious aspect of Taiwan's culture.

Buddhists have been putting more effort into spreading their faith. Over the past few years, Buddhist evangelists on television have gained popularity, and lectures on Buddhism have begun to draw large crowds. Some of the leading figures in Buddhism have even expanded their missions to North America. The famous Master Hsing-yun directed the

A Buddhist sutra.

construction of the Hsi-lai Temple in Los Angeles,

which was completed in 1988. In 1995, the Nan-Tien Temple, reputed to be the largest Buddhist temple in the southern hemisphere, was also constructed in Sydney, Australia.

Monks walk in circles and chant incantations to disperse evil and welcome good fortune.

In addition to chanting mantras and sutras, the more traditional form of worship, meditation is becoming more common among believers. Buddhist sects in general have opened centers to offer courses on meditation. The practice is becoming popular not only among worshipers, but also among politicians and businessmen, for it is a good means of relieving tension.

Buddhist organizations have also published a great deal of works on Buddhism and distributed them free of charge. Many Buddhists have actively engaged in social work, and a good example is the famous Master Cheng Yen, known here as Taiwan's "Mother Teresa." She established the Buddhist Compassion Relief Tzu-Chi Association in 1966, which now has about two million members. Over the years more than US$80 million has been donated to this organization to assist more than a million underprivileged people and those made homeless by natural disasters. Within Taiwan, this organization erected a large hospital in Hualien in 1986. Since then, it has built another hospital in Chiayi and two smaller ones in Taichung and Taipei. Abroad, it has

In the midst of Taiwan's prosperity and modernization, Buddhist lectures and prayer congregation are attracting increasing numbers of followers.

HUANG Chung-hsin

set up free health clinics in Canada and the United States and established a kidney dialysis center in Malaysia. They have sent physicians to remote areas of the Philippines nine times over the course of two years, treating over 20,000 people. In 1989, President Lee Teng-hui honored Cheng Yen for her dedication. In 1991, she also received the Roman Magsaysay Award in the Philippines (Asia's version of the Nobel Prize) for community leadership.

The Dalai Lama addressed Taiwan audiences during his ROC visit in March 1997.

The Dalai Lama serves as the leader of Tantric Buddhism. After receiving the Nobel Peace Prize, the current one visited the ROC on March 22, 1997, for five days. This trip, his first one to China since being exiled 38 years ago by the Communists, was at the invitation of Master Chinghsin with the Buddhist Association of the ROC. The Dalai Lama held two public talks, one in Kaohsiung, and the other in Taoyuan, and on March 26 he conducted a Buddhist consecration ceremony.

Some ritual items of Tantric Buddhism.

*A Taoist temple is incomplete without a censer
for burning incense.*

Taoism

Taoism developed from the philosophy of Lao Tzu, who lived during the sixth century B.C. He and others like him emphasize individual freedom, laissez-faire government, human spontaneity, and mystic power. Taoist philosophy takes his work, the Tao Te Ching, as its central text.

The themes of Taoism as a school of thought coalesced in the third century B.C., but Taoism did not become an organized religious movement until the second century A.D. The fundamental aim of the religious aspect of Taoism has been the attainment of immortality. Accordingly, people who lived in harmony with nature were said to become "immortals." Lao Tzu, founder of Taoist philosophy, eventually was deified as the head Taoist god of a huge pantheon of deified folk heroes, such as famous generals and sages. The pursuit of everlasting life

CHANG Su-ching

HUANG Chung-hsin

Incense is used for prayer and worship.

Scripts from Lukang's Tien Hou Temple.

A carriage for transporting statues of gods is pulled by faithfuls in a Taoist procession.

ultimately led to a search for concoctions which would bestow immortality, somewhat like alchemical research in Medieval Europe.

Taoism was adopted as the religion of the imperial court during the seventh through ninth centuries, and Taoist mystical elements were codified. In the ensuing centuries, the Taoist religious community became increasingly fractionalized, and Taoism became interlaced with elements of Confucianism, Buddhism, and folk religion. The particular forms of Taoism brought to Taiwan some 300 years ago (then regarded as an outlying frontier area) are considered typical of the fragmented Taoist tradition. The most distinctive feature of present practice is the worship of one's ancestors alongside Taoist deities.

During Japanese occupation (1895-1945), the colonial government implemented a policy of suppressing Taoism in Taiwan, and many religious images in Taoist temples were burned. This was partially because Taoism was associated with Chinese patriotism. To escape persecution from the Japanese, many Taoist temples registered themselves as being Buddhist and reluctantly conducted certain Buddhist ceremonies. However, after Taiwan's retrocession in 1945, such temples ceased these practices and returned to Taoism. Taoist priests from the Chinese mainland began moving

HUANG Chung-hsin

HUANG Chung-hsin

Clad in traditional Taoist gown, a Taoist priest is about to administer a temple rite.

Taoist faithfuls throng to worship the Goddess of Matsu brought from Chinese mainland's Meizhou.

HUANG Chung-hsin

The Goddess of Matsu of Meizhou is brought to Taiwan by Eva Airways.

Representations of Taoist gods and goddesses parade through the streets during a Taoist festival.

A child watches as his grandma holds out incense for prayer.

to Taiwan in increasing numbers during the Chinese civil war. In 1950, one of them, Chang En-pu, established a Taoist fellowship in Taiwan. As a 63rd generation Taoist priest of the Cheng I sect of Lung Hu Mountain, he assumed the position of this institution's director. This was the first time in Taiwan that Taoism had been organized under a central body.

In the past, much emphasis was put on constructing luxurious temples and holding frequent, lavish festivals. Today, adherents and priests pay more attention to preaching through mass media. Some Taoist leaders have turned to the strategy of using temple associations to unite various independent temples under the umbrella of a common main deity, while at the same time trying to win over spiritual leaders of small local temples and offering them guidance.

Taoist groups in Taiwan engage in extensive exchanges with their overseas counterparts. In May 1995, a group of Taoist priests from Taiwan participated in a ceremony dedicating a statue at the Peng Lai Temple in Toronto, Canada. In the summer of 1995, ROC Taoist groups also took part in cultural and academic activities in Fukien Province. Delegations from the Chinese mainland and Japan have also come to Taiwan for cultural and academic activities in recent years.

HUANG Chung-hsin

Paintings of temple door gods.

Reaching into the sky, this landmark architecture is a beacon to Catholic believers.

Catholicism

In 1626, the Spanish occupied much of northern Taiwan for 16 years. A Catholic priest, Father Martinez, accompanied the troops, bringing with him four Dominican priests from the Philippines to do missionary work. The five of them actively proselytized around the areas of what is now known as Keelung and Tamsui, converting approximately 4,000 aborigines.

The Dutch, who had occupied the area before being defeated by the Spanish, undertook a counter offensive from southern Taiwan in 1642. The Spanish were routed and driven out of Taiwan permanently; it is not known what became of their converts. In 1662, Koxinga, a Ming loyalist, retreated to Taiwan, thus, driving the Dutch off the island. This interrupted the recorded development of Christianity in Taiwan for almost 100 years.

When Jesuits came to Taiwan to map it in 1714, they found a few descendants of these early Christians who had still preserved some remnants of their forebearers' beliefs and practices. The next contact with Catholic missionaries wasn't until 1859, when Father Fernando Sainz and Father Angel Bofurull

Diego CHIU

Bishop Paul Shan of Kaohsiung diocese was elevated to cardinal by Pope John Paul II in January 1988.

traveled to Kaohsiung from the Philippines via Amoy and founded the Holy Rosary Church. This was the first Roman Catholic church in Kaohsiung and, as it is still in use, has become Taiwan's oldest extant Roman Catholic church. Father Sainz served as a missionary in the Kaohsiung, Tainan, and Pingtung areas. In 1861, he founded the Immaculate Conception Church in what today has become Wanchin Village in Wanluan.

During the Japanese occupation, Roman Catholicism experienced a relatively slow development. Some theorize that this was due to suppression by the Japanese colonial government; however, there

The well-known Holy Family Catholic Church is located on Hsinsheng South Road just opposite the Ta-an Forest Park.

HUANG Chung-hsin

is no concrete evidence to support this. By 1945, there were between 8,000 and 10,000 believers of Catholicism, 52 churches or missions, and 20 missionaries in Taiwan.

Roman Catholicism made a remarkable comeback after Taiwan's retrocession. In 1948, the number of believers stood at 13,000. When the ROC government moved to Taiwan in 1949, many priests and believers followed, infusing new strength and vigor into Taiwan's Catholic communities. Between 1953 and 1963, the number of adherents grew rapidly from 27,000 to 300,000 due to the large number of converts. The number of practicing Catholics peaked in 1969, when their numbers reached nearly 306,000 and dioceses were formed in seven cities: Taipei, Hsinchu, Taichung, Chiayi, Tainan, Kaohsiung, and Hualien. Since then, the development of Catholicism in Taiwan has reached a plateau.

On January 18, 1998, Bishop Paul Shan of the Catholic diocese in Kaohsiung was appointed car-

Diago CHIU

Around eight hundred Catholic churches dot the island.

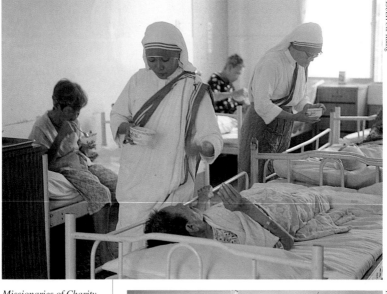

Missionaries of Charity, founded by the world-renowned Mother Teresa, looks after the sick and elderly in Taiwan.

Joyous and vibrant Catholic students pose for a photo after Sunday school.

dinal by Pope John Paul II. Shan officially assumed the new rank on February 21, when the College of Cardinals congregated at the Vatican. Shan is the only Taiwanese to be conferred the title of cardinal in the past 20 years and the fifth Chinese cardinal in the history of the Roman Catholic church. The last one from Taiwan was Cardinal Yu Pin, who was elevated to cardinal status in Nanking before he relocated to Taiwan in 1950. In the hierarchy of the Roman Catholic Church, cardinals rank just below the Pope and directly above archbishops. Electing a new pope when the exalted position becomes vacant is one of their responsibilities.

Among the leading schools founded by the Catholic church in Taiwan are Fu Jen University, the Cardinal Tien School of Nursing & Midwifery, Blessed Imelda's School, Kuangjen middle and primary schools, Providence University, Taichung Viator High School, and Wentsao Ursuline Junior College of Modern Languages. In addition, many religious bookstores, institutes, associations, and activity centers, as well as publication, radio, and television services have been set up by the Catholic church to serve the public in Taiwan.

A service held at a Protestant church. (above)
One of the many Protestant hospitals on the island. (below)

Protestantism

Christianity was introduced to Taiwan with the Protestant Dutch in 1624, with Georgius Candidius of the Reformed Church of Holland being the first successful missionary here. Candidius focused his activities on six Ping-pu aborigine communities near modern day Tainan. (The Ping-pu tribe later assimilated into the neighboring communities of Han settlers.) Robert Bunius continued Candidius' work, making southern Taiwan his home for 14 years. By the year 1643, over 6,000 aborigines had been converted, as mass conversions were typical of his evangelistic style.

A believer studies the Bible in earnest.

The earliest known missionaries were from Britain, Reverend Carstairs Douglas and Reverend H. L. Mackenzie, who came to Taiwan in 1860. They focused their efforts in northern Taiwan around the area of Tamsui and Mengchia, now called Wanhua. In 1864, Dr. James L. Maxwell was officially sent by the English Presbyterian Mission to Taiwan to preach in Tainan and southern Taiwan. In 1872, the Canadian

Presbyterian Church dispatched George L. Mackay to northern Taiwan, where he choose Tamsui as his base.

Prior to the Japanese occupation, there were 4,854 people attending 97 Protestant churches, with about 90 support staff and ministers, not to mention 13 foreign missionaries. After the Japanese gained possession of Taiwan, the colonial government exercised control over the churches, having them take in Christian groups from Japan. Missionary work by Christians among the aborigines was also strictly forbidden. When the Japanese left in 1945, Taiwan had about 238 Protestant churches and 60,000 believers.

Christianity in Taiwan boomed after the mainland fell to communism and the central government relo-

A church choir sings at a worship service.

cated to Taiwan in 1949. Churches of numerous denominations flocked to Taiwan, and the number of denominations in Taiwan jumped from just three in 1945 to approximately 40 in 1955.

Taiwan's Protestant churches experienced rapid growth between 1950 and 1964, but after the mid-1960s, their growth slowed and even did a turnaround. By 1979, the number of believers totaled around 360,000, and faith in Christianity started to make a comeback. By 1997 this figure had expanded to approximately 421,000, with nearly 2,700 protestant churches, 2,550 ministers, and 1,100 foreign missionaries in Taiwan that year.

A Protestant church in an indigenous area.

As of 1997, there were at least 65 known Protestant denominations in Taiwan. Most of which are members of the the Churches Union of the Republic of China. The largest member of the Union was the Presbyterian Church, with 421,668 members, 1,200 clergy, and 1,500 churches or congregations. The Chinese Baptist Convention, being the second largest, had 21,000 members, about 495 clergymen, and 190 churches. The third largest was the Taiwan Lutheran Church, with 6,000 members, 58 clergymen, and 53 churches. The Methodist Church in the Republic of China possessed around 2,500 members, 35 clergymen, and 25 churches. Next came the Episcopal Church, with 2,000 members, 18 clergy, and 20 churches.

Some other churches have greater numbers of believers, such as the True Jesus Church (53,125 members and 210 congregations) and the Church of Jesus Christ of Latter Day Saints (26,850 members and 50 congregations); however, for various reasons they are not members of the Churches Union of the Republic of China. Other Christian churches not having CUROC membership include the Taiwan Mission of Seventh-Day

The Unification Church rallies for a non-pornographic, non-promiscuous and AIDS-free environment.

A Christian lecturer plays a video of an elderly woman testifying her faith.

Adventists, the Jehovah's Witnesses, the Unification Church, the Mandarin Church, and the Ling Leung Church.

While mainstream Protestant churches and the Roman Catholic Church have enjoyed a head start in proselytizing, independent churches have also been growing with their fundamentalist theology, flexible administration, and self-supporting financial power. Such popular independent churches include the True Jesus Church, the Mandarin Church, and the Ling Leung Church.

The first missionaries from the Church of Jesus Christ of Latter Day Saints, also known as the Mormon Church, arrived in Taiwan in 1956. By 1963, Hu Wei-I had finished translating the Book of Mormon into Chinese, and a branch of the Mormon Church had been established locally. Since then, the Mormon faith has been spread to even the most remote reaches of Taiwan. Today the Mormon church has a local membership of more than 22,000 members.

The Mormon church has some 360 full-time missionaries, including 70 local ones, who proselytize and perform community service in Taiwan. In most areas, foreign missionaries also offer free English conversation classes to the public. There are also a handful of full-time volunteers who provide assistance to all those in need. Despite the steady rotation of foreign missionaries, Mormon churches in Taiwan are headed by local Chinese leaders.

The Jehovah's Witnesses came to Taiwan in 1950 and registered with the Ministry of the Interior in 1964. As of December 1997, they had 53 congregations around the island, with 60 foreign missionaries and more than 2,500 followers volunteering their time to lead Bible study groups.

The Unification Church, registered as the Holy Spirit Association for the Unification of World Christianity, came to Taiwan in 1971. By December 1997, it had 38 churches or congregation centers with more than 42,300 believers. On August 25, 1995, the church founder, Reverend Sun Myung Moon of Korea, and his wife, Mrs. Hak Ja Han Moon, conducted a group wedding ceremony via satellite for 8,000 couples in Taiwan.

Various international Christian organizations have established branches in Taiwan. They, along with other local groups which have surfaced, provide a network of social services to various target groups. For example, World Vision of Taiwan has been instrumental in the welfare of aborigines and children. Campus Crusade and Navigators are active on college campuses, while the Garden of Hope runs halfway houses for teenage prostitutes. The Mackay Counseling Center offers family and personal counseling, and Cathwel Service and Christian Salvation Service provides assistance for unwed mothers.

A service held at the 228 Peace Park commemorating those who died in the 228 incidents.

A Hsuan-yuan Chiao temple.

Hsuan-yuan Chiao

Hsuan-yuan Chiao was founded in Taiwan in 1957 by the 82-year-old legislator Wang Han-sheng. Wang was well-versed in the Chinese classics, including Mo Tzu, Tao-te-ching (Classic of the Way and Its Power), Nan-

Courtesy of National Palace Museum

Painting of the Yellow Emperor Hsuan-yuan.

hua-ching, Book of Changes, and such Confucian classics as the Great Learning and the Doctrine of the Mean. The etymology of this religion's name gives us a clue to Wang's thinking. The term Hsuan-yuan is in fact the name of Huangti, the Yellow Emperor, who was the original unifier of China, while chiao is the Chinese word for teachings or religion.

Wang's grief over the loss of the Chinese mainland to the Chinese communists inspired him to establish this religion. After following the ROC government to Taiwan in 1949, Wang was haunted by the question: how could a country with such a large territory as China fall into communist hands in such a short period of time? After long deliberation, he

*Altar with a statue
of the Yellow Emperor
Huangti.*

*Prayer book of
Hsuan-yuan Chiao.*

attributed the loss to the absence of national spirit, which could only be restored by a Chinese cultural renaissance.

The Faith attempts to raise people's sense of nationalism by organizing and combining China's religions and schools of thought throughout the ages, including Confucianism, Taoism, and Mohism (the teachings of Mo Tzu). The religion inherits orthodox Chinese traditions from the Yellow Emperor, Kings Wen and Wu, Confucius, and Dr. Sun Yat-sen. Adherents abide by the principles set forth in the Hsuan-yuan Chiao scriptures, the Huangti Ching, with its main tenets being reverence for heaven and one's ancestors.

Hsuan-yuan Chiao presupposes the existence of an ultimate creator—Tao or the Way. Hsuan-yuan Chiao holds that man can become divine through self-cultivation and enlightenment from the Tao, which the Huangti Ching regards as the origin of divinity. The highest state attainable in the new religion is "the union of heaven and man," where "the self is denied and yet is omnipresent." This progress can only be accomplished through self-purification, cultivation of virtuous traits, and helping others to achieve salvation.

To honor Huangti, a large-scale ceremony is held every lunar year on the ninth day of the first month.

Smaller ceremonies are held on the fifth day of the fourth month and the ninth day of the ninth month to commemorate Huangti's birthday and celebrate his ascent to heaven, respectively. Other services are performed on Sunday, known as "Laifu Day," a term derived from the Book of Changes.

The spiritual head of the religion, called the Tachungpo, is its founder Wang Han-sheng. Each of the 16 centers for worship has a leader, several preachers, and a master of rituals. The religion's largest temple is located in Tamsui.

Dressed in religious gown, a Hsuan-yuan priest administers a Sunday service.

Taipei Grand Mosque, headquarters to Muslims on the island, is located on Hsinsheng South Road opposite the Ta-an Forest Park.

Islam

It is said that Islam was introduced to China during the reign of Tai Tsung (627-649 A.D.), the second emperor of the T'ang Dynasty. Large numbers of Muslims came to China after 651A.D. from the northwest, which happens to be the home of a nomadic ethnic group called the Hui. Since the Hui

Diago CHIU

Taipei's hectic urban lifestyle makes it difficult for faithfuls to pray at dawn and dusk.

were converted to Islam, historically many Han Chinese have considered Islam an uncivilized religion unfit to follow. Later, Arab traders settled in some of the southern seaports, most notable of which was Kwangtung. After the Mongol invasion, transcontinental travel became easier due to the essential unification of such a large mass of territory under one leader—Kublai Khan. Thus, the Muslims could more easily travel to China, where they gained influence with their growing population. At that point in China's history, Muslim arts and sciences flourished, as did its medicine, astronomy, mathematics, and military science. With the decline of the Ming Dynasty, Muslims lost their standing and were persecuted during the Manchu period until the Republic of China was inaugurated in 1912.

After the fall of the Ming Dynasty in the mid-17th century, Cheng Ch'eng-kung (Koxinga) led his troops and supporters to Taiwan. Some of them were Muslim, and remnants of them are still visible in Lukang and Tamsui, among other places. By the time of Taiwan's retrocession, however, most of their descendants no longer embraced Islam; at best, some Islamic burial traditions were still observed.

Approximately 20,000 Muslims accompanied the ROC government to Taiwan in 1949; most were soldiers, civil servants, or food service workers. Two Muslim organizations re-established themselves in Taiwan to preach Islamic doctrines and construct mosques: the Chinese Muslim Association and the Chinese Muslim Youth League.

Differences in everyday habits and customs, such as those involving eating and drinking as well as religious ceremonies and activities, led to diminished contact between the Muslims and non-Muslims during the 1950s. Believers in Islam depended to a large extent on a liaison network that regularly met in a house on Lishui Street in Taipei. By the 1960s, realizing that return to the mainland would not be likely in the immediate future, Muslims in Taiwan began to engage in relatively permanent occupations. Although there was still a consider-

Women faithfuls kneel and worship in prayer.

Muslim believers attending a worship service in a mosque.

able degree of interdependence in the Islamic community, Muslims began, primarily out of professional need, to have increasingly frequent contact with Han Chinese.

Limited by a non-Muslim environment, Muslims in Taiwan today struggle to observe orthodox Islamic practices. Only a few Muslim women have adopted the traditional veil, and a handful of halal butchers and restaurants prepare meat according to the strict Islamic food observances. The busy urban lifestyle in the cities poses many constraints. For example, it is virtually impossible to keep the Islamic Sabbath which falls on Fridays, or to faithfully perform the salat, the set of prayers repeated five times a day. Besides, all prayers are conducted in Arabic which means that every adherent must master the language in spite of cultural and linguistic constraints.

Despite the restraints typical of a non-Muslim environment, three new mosques have been recently constructed in Kaohsiung, Taichung, and Lungkang to join Taipei's two in meeting the needs of Muslim adherents. These new facilities cost a total of US$2.7 million, half of which was funded by overseas donations predominantly from the Middle East.

Dome-shaped roofs are characteristics of Islamic architecture.

Diago CHIU

Li-ism, a religion founded by Yang Lai-ju,
emphasizes Chinese morals and ethics.

Li-ism

Li-ism, which could be translated as "the doctrine of order," was founded by Yang Lai-ju in the 17th century. Its creed stresses traditional Chinese morals and ethics, such as the loyalty and filial piety of Confucianism, the world salvation and forgiveness of Buddhism, and the natural way and inaction of Taoism. It is, in fact, the synthesis of Confucianism, Buddhism, and Taoism with a focus on the worship of Kuanyin (the Buddhist Goddess of Mercy). Though Li-ists worship Kuanyin, they do not reject deities of other religions. They believe that providence may be revealed in the form of other deities and prophets, such as Buddha, Christ, or Mohammed.

Li-ism adherents must strictly abstain from smoking, drinking, and taking drugs. Like in Buddhism, incense, flowers, and fruit are used during worship. Li-ism adherents can eat meat except when fasting, or the birthday of Kuanyin which falls on the 19th day of the second month of the lunar calendar. Li-ists abide by the great law of Li-ism called Fa Pao Tieh Wen (precious and official decrees), written by Yang.

Li-ists worship Kuanyin, the Buddhist Goddess of Mercy.

A woman believer sounds a drum for peace and favorable weather.

TSUH Tse-jung

TSUH Tse-jung

Yang was a Ming Dynasty scholar who was appointed by the Manchu court to be magistrate of Mei Hsien in Kwangtung Province, but the patriot turned it down flatly. Alarmed that the Ming Dynasty fall was due to lack of ethics and morals, Yang sold his house and traveled throughout Shangtung, Hopei and Honan. He sought to forge alliances with the patriots in China to overthrow the Manchu court.

During his travels in China, Yang experienced several "miraculous phenomena," which eventually caused him to set his goals even higher from national revival to world salvation. The History of Li-ism describes how Kuanyin, the sacred personage of Li-ism, revealed herself twice to Yang and presented him with the great doctrine and sacred classics, respectively.

Afterwards, Master Yang led a reclusive life at Shui-lan Cave in Hopei Province, cultivating his mind and

Li-ist monks conduct a ceremony with offerings to the gods.

spirit. At age 81, having formulated Li-ism's ideological system for world salvation, Yang ended his life of solitude to preach the doctrine of Li-ism. He died, reputedly, at the age of 133. By then, he had written the classics, creed, commandments, and rituals of Li-ism.

Before the Chinese communists took over the mainland, more than 14 million adherents of Li-ism had received tien li (baptism), and there were 4,800-odd temples dedicated to Li-ism in and around Peking, Tientsin, and Shanghai.

Li-ist clergies pose for a photo in traditional clothing.

Following the fall of the mainland, many adherents came to Taiwan with the ROC government. The Association of Li-ism was officially re-established in Taiwan in 1950. The Li-ism General Council and main temple were established in western Taipei at Hsimenting. Covering an area of 3,126 pings, the Tang palace-style temple was built from 2,000-year-old pinewood without the use of a single nail.

Today, Li-ism has spread to Korea, Hong Kong, Japan, the Philippines, and even the United States. In 1952, Sheng-li College was established in Taipei for Li-ists to study the classics. This institution also publishes two magazines—On Loyalty and Filial Piety, and Enlightenment on Li-ism.

The Tenrikyo headquarters are located in the Yuanshan area of Taipei.

Root TANG

Root TANG

Clad in religious gowns, Tenrikyo monks perform a ceremony at a temple.

Tenrikyo

Tenrikyo was founded in Japan in 1838 by Miki Nakayama. The daughter of a peasant family in Sammaiden, Nara Prefecture, Miki was visited by God the Parent when she was 41. From then on, she spoke and acted on behalf of God the Parent, advising people to abide by God's will so they can lead a life of joy.

To lead such a life, people must root out the concept that they are in control of their own destiny. All ideas of opposing God's will are regarded as "dust," and only when the dust is swept away can mankind be saved. Tenrikyo followers worship God the Parent (called Tenri-O-no-Mikoto in Japanese). As this deity is said to have created the world and all of mankind, people should treat one another as brothers and sisters.

The Tenrikyo Church is headquartered at Tenri City in Nara Prefecture and services are held at Jiba. Jiba is the place they believe to be the origin of man, hence it is considered the source of universal salvation and the home of all mankind. For this reason, the district is called Oyasato (ancestral home), and it is also the destination of many Tenrikyo pilgrimages.

Brochures and booklets on Tenrikyo.

Root TANG

Several large-scale ceremonies are held at the Tenrikyo head-quarters. For instance, the Grand Autumn Service held on October 26th commemorates the founding of Tenrikyo. The founder's birthday is celebrated on April 18, while the Grand Spring Service on January 26th commemorates the day she passed away.

Before performing a religious rite, a Tenrikyo follower must clap his hands four times and then chant the phrase "Sweep away evil and save mankind, Tenri-o-no-mikoto" 21 times. During the grand services held every month, the worshipers dance to music accompanied by sacred songs, which were choreographed and composed by the foundress herself. Other forms of worship are conducted daily every morning and evening.

In the Chinese mainland, Tenrikyo temples were first set up in Peiping (Peking), Tientsin, Chingtao, Shanghai, Nanking, Amoy (Hsiamen), Mongolia, and Northeast China. The religion was later introduced to Taiwan during the Japanese occupation.

Tenrikyo stresses respect for one's ancestors, filial piety, self-cultivation, and service to mankind. Thus, it resembles traditional Chinese ethics and the concept of universal brotherhood. The religion was therefore readily accepted in Taiwan, where it continued to develop and was formally recognized by the Ministry of the Interior in 1973.

The Tenrikyo headquarters, a palace-like building with a golden-colored roof and white walls, is located in the Yuanshan area of Taipei. It also has two main branches in Chiayi and Changhua counties and 61 smaller places of worship all over the island. On the tenth of each month, followers worship at the temples wearing black kimonos with the characters for Tenrikyo embroidered on them in white.

Tenrikyo followers on a tour mission to console and comfort the needy and the sick.

天理教聖勞隊

TSUH Tse-juang

A family outing among Baha'i followers.

Baha'is gatherings are informal, without a clergy, and concentrate on free discussion.

Baha'i

"He hath manifested unto men the Day Stars of His divine guidance...and hath ordained the knowledge of these sanctified Beings to be identical with the knowledge of His own self. Whoso recognizeth them hath recognized God.

"If thou wilt observe with discriminating eyes, thou wilt behold Them all abiding in the same tabernacle, soaring in the same heaven, seated upon the same throne, uttering the same speech and proclaiming the same Faith." From the writings of Baha'u'llah.

Baha'is uphold that during the progress of human civilization, God has sent messengers such as Krishna, Moses, Buddha, Jesus, and Mohammed to teach His pur-

Baha'is believe that the family is the foundation of human society.

Courtesy of the National Spiritual Assembly of the Baha'is of Taiwan

Bahai's communities conduct functions often focus on social issues.

pose. Baha'is believe that God's most recent messenger and the promised one of all religions is Baha'u'llah, whose name means the "Glory of God."

The Faith was founded in Iran in 1844 by the "Bab," who prophesied that a great new teacher would come after him. This great teacher was Baha'u'llah, who declared His station in 1863.

Before his death in 1892, Baha'u'llah appointed his eldest son, Abdu'l-Baba, as the sole interpreter of his teachings and the center of his covenant. Abdu'l-Baha passed on that duty to his grandson, Shoghi Effendi, who became the guardian of the Baha'i Faith and interpreter of Baha'u'llah's teachings. Shogi developed a worldwide Administrative Order and appointed 27 individuals as the "Hands of the Cause of God" to promote and protect the Baha'i Faith.

Six years after Shogi's death, the Universal House of Justice was established, making it the highest governing body of the Baha'i Faith. It consists of nine members who are elected by the National Spiritual Assemblies all over the world. This body may be consulted on any issue, as it guides the entire Baha'i community within the light and framework of the teachings of the Baha'u'llah.

The National Spiritual Assembly of each country is elected by delegates at an annual national convention. Its nine members advise on and preside over the spiritual affairs of that particular nation.

The Baha'i Faith reached the Far East in the early 1900s. In 1924 Ms. Martha Root, an American journalist, went to Kwangtung and introduced the Baha'i faith to Dr. Sun Yat-sen. She later wrote articles for a number of local gazettes, spoke at many universities, and introduced the religion to other Chinese leaders.

The first convert from Taiwan was introduced to the Baha'i Faith while studying in the United States in 1949. Taiwan's second contact with this religion occurred in 1954, when an Iranian couple came from mainland China as missionaries and established Taiwan's first Baha'i center in Tainan. Currently, the local Baha'i headquarters, the National Spiritual Assembly of the Baha'is of Taiwan, is located in Taipei.

Books on the Baha'i Faith.

Baha'i communities all over the world target urgent social issues of each region. For instance, in Taiwan the local Baha'i assemblies have singled out environmental protection as their main area of concern. Since 1990, the Baha'i community has launched joint projects with government organizations to promote environmental awareness amongst kindergarten and elementary schools around the country. Baha'is visit these schools and organize games designed to teach basic principles of environmental protection. The Baha'i community has produced around 30 radio programs on environmental issues. It has also published a book on environmental education in collaboration with the Homemakers' Union and Foundation.

Baha'is believe that all people are the children of a single Creator, and that the different races are like flowers of many colors in one garden; though different, all should co-exist in harmony. To realize world peace, everyone must purge themselves of all forms of prejudice, seek "the truth" on their own, and not be superstitious. They believe that consultation is a dynamic process which can assist them to find the truth and solve conflicts.

Baha'is also maintain that the family is the foundation of human society and that marriage is a means for both partners to develop spiritually. Other tenets include equality between men and women, compulsory education for all, the need for science and religion to develop in parallel, loyalty to one's government, and abidance by the law.

An unusual feature of the Baha'i Faith is the absence of a clergy. In its stead, informal public discussions are the norm, during which participants discuss their faith with each other and interested friends. Baha'is also meet regularly every 19 days at special gatherings for prayer, community consultation, and social activities.

To become a Baha'i, there is no ceremony—one simply signs a card declaring one's faith; the important thing is to recognize the fact that truth exists. Once one becomes a Baha'i there are certain obligations to observe. For instance, one must pray and read the Holy Writings daily, fast from sunrise to sunset between March 2-21, consider work as a religious duty, and contribute to the Baha'i Fund.

HUANG Chung-hsin

Baha'is believe all people are the children of a single creator and the different races are like flowers of many colors in a garden.

T'ienti Teachings expect believers to first prove themselves to family and country before devoting themselves to the path of heavenly salvation.

The magnificent T'ienti Teachings' temple complex.

T'ienti Teachings

T'ienti Teachings, or Lord of Universe Church, was founded by Lee Yu-chieh in the mid-1980s after he broke away from Tien Te Chiao. Born in 1901 in Kiangsu Province, Lee became a disciple of Master Hsiao Chang-ming, founder of Tien Te Chiao, in 1930. Three years later, he set up an Institute for the Study of Religious Philosophy in Shanghai. He worked to transform people through the Twenty Words of Truth, meditation, and cosmic Ch'i healing. Later he completed his *A New System of Religious Philosophy*, also known as *The Ultimate Realm*, which became T'ienti's primary text.

A banner of T'ienti Teachings.

During the War of Resistance against the Japanese, the Lord of Heaven communicated with Lee, who then moved with his wife and four sons to Mt. Hua in western China to pray and meditate. In 1949, Lee was advised by his teacher's teacher, Yun-lung Chih-sheng, to move with the ROC government to Taiwan. In 1951, he set up the *Independence Evening Post*, an independent and non-partisan paper. Feeling threatened by the possibility of a com-

Books introducing T'ienti Teachings.

HUANG Chung-hsin

Followers of T'ienti Teachings are especially concerned about nuclear war and their prayers often revolve round this issue.

munist invasion and even nuclear war, he prayed day and night, appealing to the Lord of Heaven for permission to resurrect T'ienti Teachings on earth and save mankind. According to Lee, the Lord of Heaven granted his request on December 21, 1980, and designated Lee as Chief Envoy on earth to resurrect the faith.

T'ienti Teachings draws upon some of China's oldest religious traditions and venerates the Lord of Heaven (T'ienti)—who is believed to rule the universe and be none other than God (in the Christian sense). The Lord of Heaven created the universe and offered salvation through his messengers.

The T'ienti Teachings, described in *The Ultimate Realm*, advocates magnanimity through kindness and stresses the co-existence between the spiritual and material worlds. The religion demands that one first prove oneself to one's family and country before becoming devoted to the study of heavenly ways of salvation. The ultimate goal of this religion is a world of universal love regardless of one's race or creed.

Emphasis is placed on cultivating one's moral self, and Twenty Words of Truth, which serve as "required daily homework" for adherents. These Twenty Words of Truth are *Chung* (loyalty), *Shu* (forgiveness), *Lien* (incorruptibility), *Ming* (insight), *Teh* (virtue), *Cheng* (rectitude), *Yi* (justice), *Hsin* (trustworthiness), *Ren* (forbearance), *Kung* (fairness), *Po* (philanthropy), *Hsiao* (filial piety), *Jen* (benevolence), *Tz'u* (compassion), *Chueh* (awareness), *Chieh* (moderation, fidelity), *Chien* (frugality), *Chen* (Truthfulness), *Li* (Propriety), and *Ho* (harmony).

T'ienti Teachings has four commandments. The first states, "thou shall not harm others, take revenge, disregard divine teachings, or covet wealth." The second commands, "thou shall not deceive others, be promiscuous, arrogant, quarrelsome or contentious." The third requires, "thou shall not infringe upon other peoples' freedom, disobey the moral code, or misjudge right and wrong." The fourth demands, "thou shall not humiliate the exalted ones or violate church rules." Worshiping the Lord of Heaven in all sincerity and refraining from superstition and idol worship are both required. Also emphasized are mutual respect, the pursuit of truth, and amity among religions. Basic practice also includes reflection and repentance, meditation, filling out "striving cards," and chanting the Grand Orison, in which the Lord is invoked.

The fact that followers of T'ienti Teachings are especially concerned about nuclear war can be seen through two of their current missions. The first is to diminish the danger of worldwide nuclear war. The second is to secure Taiwan as the base for the revival of T'ienti Teachings and promote the peaceful reunification of China, thereby, further ensuring peace for the world. Since its founding, 52 temples with 138 clergymen have been established, with most of them concentrated in Taipei, Taichung, Tainan, Pingtung, and Hualien.

T'ienti Teachings sponsors two colleges in Taiwan and runs two affiliated organizations to conduct philanthropic work: the Institute of Research on Religious Philosophy and the Red Heart Society. The former engages in the research of religion and philosophy, while the latter carries out social welfare and charity services. Religious centers have also been built outside of the Republic of China: a Principle Hall in Los Angeles and two Original Halls in Tokyo.

A Tien Te Chiao with images of the Master of the Universe flanked by the Buddhist Goddess of Mercy on the right and Wang Ti-ching on the left. (above) Faithfuls chant scriptures in their prayers. (below)

Tien Te Chiao

Founded in mainland China in 1923, Tien Te Chiao is a synthesis of the two major philosophical religions of China, Confucianism and Taoism, and three other religions of the world, Buddhism, Christianity, and Islam. Its beliefs and disciplines apply not only to this world, but also to the heavens and the underworld. These reflect the structural framework of the universe, without which the universe would surely collapse in chaos.

According to the religious annals of Tien Te Chiao, in 1894, the "master of the universe" descended from heaven to this world in a merciful attempt to help mankind avoid impending disasters. The master is the deified personification of the formless mass from which the cosmos was shaped.

Tien Te Chiao's founder, Hsiao Chang-ming, was born in southwest China and began preaching at the age of seven, but no one would believe the little boy. Then one night his original being, or celestial spirit, appeared in his dreams, giving him the gift to heal and directing him to reach the people through medical services. His talent for healing attracted much attention. Some ten years later, his

節 博 正 忠
儉 孝 義 恕　廿
眞 仁 信 廉　字
禮 慈 忍 明　大
和 覺 公 德　道

The Twenty Principles of Tien Te Chiao.

A Tien Te priest beats a wooden "fish" block and chants prayers while performing a rite.

comprehension of the heavens, the human world, and the underworld earned him the title Celestial Worthy.

In 1923, he wrote out twenty characters representing the principles to which adherents of Tien Te Chiao were to strictly adhere throughout their lives: loyalty, forbearance, honesty, openness, virtue, uprightness, righteousness, faith, endurance, fairness, universal love, filial piety, benevolence, kindness, consciousness, moral integrity, frugality, truth, courtesy, and harmony. Once believers have disciplined themselves through adherence to the 20 principles, they start learning how to meditate under the guidance of their masters. They are instructed to search for their original being, which is free and untainted from worldly ties and yearnings. Adherents also practice various methods of self-cultivation, health maintenance, faith healing, and acupuncture.

After the Nationalist government relocated to Taiwan, a disciple named Wang Ti-ching moved to Taiwan and began to spread the religious discipline in Kaohsiung. Due to his efforts to heal the sick, in 1966 the Psychic Healing Research Association of China was founded. Other centers for worship and medical services were subsequently set up throughout the island.

The general headquarters of Tien Te Chiao was established in 1974. Wang passed away later that year and was given special acclimations for introducing Tien Te Chiao to Taiwan. Religious responsibilities then fell on the shoulders of Chin Shu-te, who headed *Jeau Ming* magazine. In April 1989, Tien Te Chiao was recognized officially under the Civic Organizations Law. Two months later the Republic of China Headquarters of Tien Te Chiao was established as the combination of a religious order and social organization.

Today, in Tien Te Chiao halls of worship, a statue of the master of the universe is placed at the altar, flanked by the Buddhist goddess of Mercy (Kuanyin) on its right, and Wang Ti-ching on its left. Worshipers carry out solemn rituals, while scriptures are chanted and incense burnt. Adherents are required to worship their deities and study the scriptures on a daily basis.

To enter this faith, one must be at least 20 years old and be recommended by two members of the Tien Te Chiao headquarters. Those accepted are initiated in a ceremony conducted by an enlightened master. Only then can they be taught the various methods of self-cultivation, health maintenance, and psychic healing, including the "formless needle," "golden light," "gold elixir," and "palm light."

One of Tien Te Chiao's publications.

Faithfuls throng to a religious ceremony at the inauguration of a new I-kuan Tao temple. (above) I-kuan Tao's basic writings, religious observances, and moral precepts are all embedded in traditional Chinese culture. (below)

I-kuan Tao

A rough translation of I-kuan Tao could be "the First and Constant Way." The name connotes I-kuan Tao's nature as a spiritual doctrine that draws upon both traditional Chinese teachings and each of the world's major religions. I-kuan Tao is a modern, syncretic faith, and the third most popular religion in Taiwan.

According to I-kuan Tao practitioners, this religion attempts to identify common principles underlying Taoism, Buddhism, Christianity, Islam, Judaism, and Hinduism. They also believe that by uncovering a single set of universal truths, the " increasing chaos" of modern times can be defeated and the world can live in peaceful harmony. As such, they believe in a god above all other gods—Ming-ming Shang-ti (the God of Clarity).

Books on I-kuan Tao.

The doctrine of San Pao (three treasures) is passed on to new members by a special priest during secret initiation rites. The proper receipt of the three treasures signifies that the recipient has obtained the Tao (teachings of heaven) and that his name has been reserved in heaven and erased from

I-kuan Tao followers often provide social services such as free medical check-ups and relief to the needy and disaster victims. (pages 68 & 69)

the lists in hell. Upon death, the recipient will ascend straight to heaven without having to endure the Buddhist and Hindu cycles of transmigration.

As a religion, I-kuan Tao is highly accessible to the Chinese people. One reason for its rapid spread throughout China over the years is that, although I-kuan Tao claims to be a universal religion, its basic writings, religious observances, and moral precepts are all embedded in traditional Chinese culture. I-kuan Tao is therefore readily understandable to the average Chinese person.

While I-kuan Tao boasts large numbers of followers in Australia, Canada, the United States, South Africa, France, Italy, and elsewhere, it is widely embraced only by the overseas Chinese communities in these countries. A cause (or perhaps an effect) of this phenomenon is that only limited fragments of I-kuan Tao scripture have been translated into non-Chinese languages.

I-kuan Tao adherents more or less follow the rituals of traditional Confucianism and engage in ancestor worship. Services are usually held at family shrines and are aimed at both cultivating personal character and maintaining family relations—two key concepts in Chinese culture. The faithful believe that by increasing the number of I-kuan Tao temples, they can bring the Buddhist "Western Paradise" to this world, while creating in it brotherhood and universal love as envisioned by Confucian teachings.

The goodness of cultivating a virtuous character and the grace of a life of service are key tenets in I-kuan Tao doctrine. This being so, adherents devote a great deal of resources to social work. This service ethic is closely related to the order's tradition that believers should "give their heart to the universe and dedicate their lives to humanity."

An I-kuan Tao follower should abstain from drinking alcohol and strive every day to respect truth and law. Meanwhile, they should endeavor to put into practice the I-kuan Tao ideals of benevolence, righteousness, courtesy, wisdom, and faith.

Courtesy of I-kuan Tao

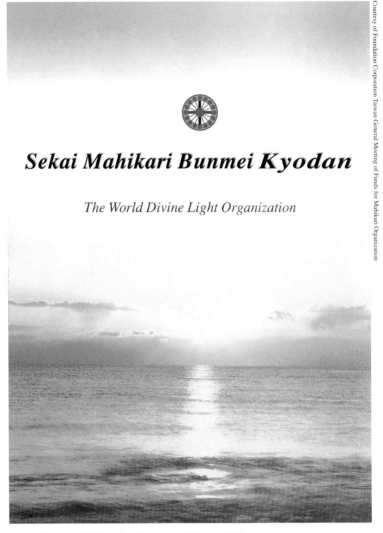

Sekai Mahikari Bunmei Kyodan

The World Divine Light Organization

Founded in Japan, Mahikarikyo first came to Taiwan in 1983.

Mahikarikyo

Mahikarikyo was founded in 1959 by Yosikazu Okada, a former Japanese army officer born on February 27, 1901. In 1941, Okada suffered from caries of his spinal cord, and was told by doctors that he had only three years to live. However, the power of his faith healed him completely. He subsequently invested all his family assets into various businesses, but the loss of his factory from an air raid left him heavily in debt.

A Mahikarikyo religious illustration.

In 1959, Yosikazu finished paying off his debt. On February 27 of the same year, he received his first divine visitation, "Heaven's time has come. Arise and take the name Kotama. The World shall become a harsh place." When Okada asked with what name should he praise Him, the divine entity said, "Call me Su-God. All the races of humanity shall embrace this name."

Mahikarikyo believes that anyone can acquire healing powers by taking a three-day seminar on the Spiritual Art of Divine Light.

According to Mahikarikyo, Su-God has had a variety of names throughout time. These have included the Sun Goddess Amaterasu Ohomikami from Shinto, Seikannon (Avalokitesvara) from Buddhism, Yahweh from Christianity, and Allah from Islam. He is the First Cause and central God, the Creator of all things.

In the past Su-God revealed to a small number of saints and holy ones, the Mahikari-no-waza (also called the Tekazashi), the spiritual art of divine light and a secret of Heaven called the "Teaching of the Righteous Law." Su-God now enlightens the people through the Oshienushi-sama—those to whom he speaks.

As instructed by Su-God, in August 1959, Kotama established the L. H. Company of Sun Light Children. Similarlly, in 1963 he set up the Sekai Mahikari Bunmei Kyodan (The World Divine Light Organization).

Kotama passed away on June 23, 1974, and was succeeded by the second Oshienushi Sekae Sekiguchi, or Reverend Seiho, who had served under Kotama since 1959. Reverend Seiho worked to fulfill the late Kotama's wishes by building the Suza World Main Shrine in Amagi on the Izu Peninsula; construction was completed in August 1987. Upon his death on January 3, 1994, Seiho's eldest son, Sakae Sekiguchi (or Reverend Seisho), succeeded him to become the third Oshienushi-sama by divine decree.

The Teachings of the Righteous Law:

The divine messages by Su-God are called the "Teachings of Divine Truth and Righteous Law." The Oshienushi-sama published two books on some of Su-God's teachings entitled Go-Seigen (Holy Words) and Norigoto-shui (the Holy Prayer Book).

The teachings of Divine Truth and Righteous Law reveal to humankind the secrets of the heavenly world. God did not allow Moses, Buddha, or Jesus to reveal these secrets, even though they may have had such knowledge. The five great religions of the world were given but a slight glimpse of the teachings. This is the reason that the other world and such matters have always been enigmatic and caused misunderstandings and forced interpretations by worshipers of other faiths.

The adherents of this faith believe that their Teachings will lead all people to the coming Holy Twenty-First Century; the next century will bring with it the attainment of happiness to all people regardless of race, nationality, religion, age, or sex.

Mahikari-no-waza
(The Spiritual Art of Divine Light)

The first Oshienushi-sama Kotama held his palms up to people (Tekazashi) as commanded and created miracles by healing those on the verge of death. Thus, Mahikarikyo teaches that the spiritual world can negatively affect our health, human relationships, and economic circumstances. Nevertheless, the Tekazashi (the Spiritual Art of Divine Light) can remove these factors and allow people to find happiness.

The Bible gives accounts of Jesus curing the sick, while ancient Buddhist sutras contain pictures of Buddha saving sentient beings by holding his palms up to them.

As the Bible states that "God is light" and the Buddhist scriptures also mention an "infinite light," in a similar fashion Shinto professes its Sun Goddess. In every culture, the divine has been said to be expressed through light. Tekazashi is said to be the light of deliverance given to us by God, thus, demonstrating from time immemorial that "God is light."

Today humanity is facing the possibility of extinction, and wherever you look there are strange and incurable diseases. But yet there is still hope, for God has granted all people the art of salvation (the Spiritual Art of Divine Light) to save themselves and humankind through the Oshienushi-sama. Anyone—regardless of race, nationality, religion, sect, age, or sex—can learn the Spiritual Art of Divine Light by taking a simple three-day seminar.

Although Mahikarikyo was first introduced into Taiwan in 1983, the religion was not formally registered with the Ministry of the Interior until April 8, 1996. It was registered under the title "Foundation Corporation Taiwan General Meeting of Funds for Mahikari Organization," with the organization's headquarters located on Sungchiang Road, Taipei, Taiwan (Tel: 2567-0736).

By June 1998, the religion already had more than 3,750 believers, as well as seven shrines located around the island. These shrines—which are located in Taipei, Tienmou, Taichung, Wuch'i, Kaohsiung, Pingtung, and Fenglin—each conduct a meeting once per month and an intermediate seminar once per year for the faithful. Mahikarikyo advocates respect for nature, love amongst human beings, and spiritual purification through religious teachings.

Religious Groups and Activity in the ROC (1997)

Religions	Total (1997)	Buddhism	Taoism	Catholicism	Protestantism
Temples and Churches	16,431	3,938	8,557	816	2,678
Clergy	124,109	9,239	33,200	2,822	2,549
Believers (thousand)	11,821	4,863	4,505	304	421
Foreign Missionaries	1,919	47		706	1,071
Monasteries and Seminaries	88	31	2	7	38
Universities	17	5		3	8
Colleges	28	3	1	15	9
High Schools	40	4		27	9
Elementary Schools	21			10	11
Kindergartens	455	43	59	271	44
Nurseries	37	28		7	2
Orphanages	11	6		4	1
Retirement Homes	18	5	3	4	1
Rehabilitation Centers	4			3	1
Centers for the Retarded	25	1		23	1
Handicapped Welfare Institutions	7			5	2
Institutions for Proselytizing	233	58	22	103	
Hospitals	52	3	1	15	12
Clinics	70	3	19	17	14
Libraries	176	113	16	39	1
Publishing Houses	180	30	9	7	97
Publications	281	24	160		57

-yuan Chiao	Li-ism	Tenrikyo	Baha'i	T'ienti Teachings	I-kuan Tao	Tien Te Chiao	Mahikarikyo
18	128	145	2	52	87	4	
109	629	420	2	133	74,946	30	
136	152	22	12	211	942	200	1
		30	53	5			6
1	3			2	4		
				1			
	3			1	34		
1					4		
8	11			2		22	7
					21		
3	6				8		
				1		2	
1	1		1	2	30	1	
		3			32	3